A WORD ON *Love*

DISCOVER THE POWER OF ALLOWING GOD TO LOVE THROUGH YOU

Bishop Ruth W. Smith, Ph.D.

EWE
Excellent Way
Enterprises

Scripture references are taken from the
King James Version of the Holy Bible
unless otherwise noted.

Publisher:
Excellent Way Enterprises
P. O. Box 421
Lithonia, GA 30058
www.excellentwayenterprises.com

First Edition
ISBN: 978-0-692-00405-0

Library of Congress Control Number: 2009931317

Printed in the United States of America.

Dedication

To my Lord, Jesus Christ. Thank you for your love, for the inspiration to teach about love and for your being the greatest example of love.

To my late husband, friend and co-laborer in the ministry, Archbishop Jimmie L. Smith, for loving me and showing so many how to love according to the Word of God.

◆

Contents

Contents (continued)

Foreword

Bishop Ruth Smith continues the trilogy of John the Beloved's three epistles in the book you now hold in your hands. Listen to a passage from John as translated in *The Message Bible*:

> *My beloved friends, let us continue to love each other since love comes from God. Everyone who loves is born of God and experiences a relationship with God. The person who refuses to love doesn't know the first thing about God, because God is love— so you can't know him if you don't love. This is how God showed his love for us: God sent his only Son into the world so we might live through him. This is the kind of love we are talking about—not that we once upon a time loved God, but that he loved us and sent his Son as a sacrifice to clear away our sins and the damage they've done to our relationship with God.* (1 John 4:7-10, *The Message Bible*)

This truth is unpacked by Bishop Ruth in all three aspects—loving God, loving ourselves, and loving others. In a marvelous way, she explains each, as well as describes the intricate and inner weavings in this dance of love. Bishop Ruth helps us understand both the strength and fragility of love in all its applications.

Further, she reminds us that with God's love, we gain balance in our lives. We can remain strong enough to keep life's negative forces at bay, and if and when they appear, we are strong enough to handle them. We are less likely to accept false love, and even if we do, we are strong enough to recognize what it is (false love and weakness of the flesh) and make appropriate choices and changes.

This book packs a powerful message for those who seek love in all the wrong places and offers them a better way to gain and hold onto real transforming love. This magnificent love channeled though God is love spelled with a capital "L." This sets it apart from all other declarations and professions of love.

With this book, we hold in our hands perhaps that which is the number one need in our lives—that is, to experience unconditional love and acceptance. The need for love appears as early as birth and remains until we reach the highest level of love, which is God's eternal and everlasting love. The writer shares the importance of seeking relationships with people who challenge us to seek God's love first and to seek and accept the right kind of love.

The thesis of the book as discussed by Bishop Ruth is that a common and mistaken belief about love is that we can find healthy and lasting love without loving and seeking God first. Oftentimes, the illusive and fleeting type of love is the kind that we seek. However, we usually find great disappointments and heartaches from this kind of love. This is because we are creating our own standards for love instead of following God's standards for this important emotion in our lives. Bishop Smith has shared that we must first open ourselves up before God in order that this strong and enduring love can flow from Him through us. Securing love this way gives God a chance to place his Holy protection and approval on love before it enters our hearts.

Neil Sedaka sang "Love Will Keep Us Together" and a few years later Tina Turner sang "What's Love Got to Do with It?"—in *A Word on Love,* Bishop Smith will lead you on a journey through both these extremes and bring you back to God-centric love.

Dr. Samuel R. Chand
Samuel Chand Consulting
(samchand@samchand.com)

Preface

Several months ago, one of my family members taught a lesson comparing the love of a mother to the love of God. He talked about all the things he went through as a youth and how his mother walked through those difficult times with him. As he was speaking, I kept thinking to myself, *"What would make a mother go through that, persevere like that? What would make a mother hold on so tightly when she really wants to dust her hands?"* The more I listened to and heard what he said, the more I thought to myself, *"It is the love of God."* The love a mother or a father has for their children cannot simply be a natural human characteristic. It must be created by something much greater than limited human emotion. There must be more to it. There is more to it. When our fleshly selves push us to cease loving and we no longer feel like giving love, God helps us to keep on loving.

This lesson led me to take a deeper look at the love of God and how awesome His love is. As a Pastor, I began to realize that a lot of things we're trying to teach to the body of Christ right now (how to do this, how to do that, how *not* to do this, and how *not* to do that) would be so much easier if we began with this most significant phenomenon.

God said to me, "*Ruth, the most important thing you've got to teach the people is to love me first – to love me with all their hearts.*" He said, "*If people will just love me with all their hearts – more than family, more than money, more than life itself – it will be easier for them to walk according to my Word and to love others the way they should love them.*"

You have to love God with everything within you, and that's really the only thing we have to get straight in our hearts.

I must confess that many years ago I did not consider myself a "loving person." I remember observing and admiring those who were seemingly loving and I wondered how they lived their everyday lives, speaking kind words and doing kind deeds. I marveled at how others responded – the smiles, the embraces, and the lingering "love looks." These observations really touched my heart.

Now, I do not use the responses of others to judge the worth of my actions when it comes to love. Instead, I seek to be led by God. I thank Him for the understanding that what matters most is my being led by the Spirit of God. Only when I allow Him to show His love for others through me do I truly love them.

You may be saying to yourself, "*I just can't believe a person in the ministry hasn't always been loving.*" Understand, I wasn't satisfied with where I was. I wanted to do better – to walk in God's perfect will concerning love. To manifest His will in my life required me to allow God to sanction love in and through me. I made a decision to yield to the Lord. I surrendered my personality, my ways of thinking, my habits, and my understanding in exchange for God's way of loving. Today, I am a much better person because of my decision to surrender to God and His way of loving others. Additionally, I now set a better example for others to love through God.

All too often, I tried to love people from my own nature – giving them the love I thought they should have, and saying the things that I thought they wanted and needed to hear. Furthermore, when I loved through my own nature, I grew tired easily and oftentimes found myself getting weary.

When God loves through us, sometimes others may not have a "fuzzy wuzzy" feeling on the inside. At first, they may feel uncomfortable or inconvenienced because His love shows them their disobedience or sin. This difficult guidance is sometimes called "tough love." However, such love can move them to live according to His word. Thank God for deliverance by the revelation of His Word! Knowing and sharing His love is the path upon which we can journey to a joyous and loving life. It is that journey I hope to share with you in this book. If you can relate to my journey, get ready for your deliverance. God has a Word for you.

A Word on Love covers the different aspects of love found in the Word of God. The scriptural and personal references are meant to lead you to more purposeful relationships with God, family members, friends, and others who cross your path.

I begin with why loving God is so important and why this is the foundation to loving anyone else. Jesus states in John 15 that we should abide in His love so that His joy can remain in us. *"Abiding in His love"* means staying in love with Him. Are you still in love with Jesus? Has the fire gone out? Do you need to rekindle the flame today? If your love for Christ has dwindled, this is where you need to make your first steps towards change. Otherwise, you will never be able to love anyone else quite the right way, and your joy may be stolen away from you.

Next, I help you to understand that we need to get one thing straight - Just one thing! The one thing that we must do is to love God with everything in us – all of our heart, our soul, and our mind. Matthew 22 demands it. This is the first and most important commandment, and this is where you should start. When you do this, some things can be avoided, eliminated, and even made easier. Your love for

God will lead you to want to please Him by walking according to His Word by faith. When you love God with all your heart, you will love Him enough to gravitate to the Word and to gravitate to a lifestyle that compliments who God says you are.

From there, we consider how to love yourself God's way. The Bible states that you should love your neighbor as yourself. If you know how to love yourself appropriately, then you will know how to love your neighbor. It's important to know what the Word says about *who* you are and *whose* you are. Even when you are negatively affected by your upbringing, financial status, fear, or even your health, you will be able to push out the old way of thinking and replace it with what God says. When we read 1 John 4, we find that *"Greater is He that is in you than he who is in the world."* It doesn't matter what's going on with you, for God's path is greater, and through Him, you can overcome any challenges. You will find out that in God, you are victorious and that you are perfect in His sight. Because God sees us through the blood of Jesus, we do not have to be sin-conscious; we can be God-conscious!

I close out the book with a word about loving your neighbor. How can we say that we love God (whom we cannot see) when we do not love our neighbor or others whom we can see? Furthermore, we should not only love the neighbors who love us in return, but we should also love the neighbors we consider to be our enemies. On one hand, I will show you in Exodus 12 how God gave the Children of Israel favor with the Egyptians – their enemies – by allowing the Egyptians to give them silver, gold, and other articles before leaving bondage in Egypt. On the other hand, I also share why it's important for you to make provisions for others, according to Proverbs 3.

Allowing God to love *through* you, which is the right way to love, will transform your life and all the lives of those you share it with. This way of loving has transformed my life, the lives of my family and moved me spiritually to a new place with God.

Bishop Ruth W. Smith

◆

1

Why Love?

One Myth about Love

One of the myths about love is that people are born with a natural ability to love. No one is born naturally loving, and if the truth were told, we are born quite the opposite. From the moment we take our first breath, our natural inclination is to be sure that our own needs are met. We cry demanding, selfish cries from a young age, and we continue doing just that throughout our lifetimes. However, some people have more accommodating personalities, and some are kinder than others, however, true love can only come from God.

True love comes to us through God. If our love is not founded on God's *agape* love, which is so utterly unconditional and amazing, it will always falter. We will always get tired, we will always get weary, and we will always want to give up on any kind of relationship if it's not rooted and grounded in the love of God. Why? Because deep down, as much as we think we love others, we cannot possibly love them on our own the way that God intends love to be.

A husband and wife's relationship won't last if the two can't get past their egos or if they cannot maintain their relationship after that dizzying romantic feeling of being "in love" wears off. If we remain steadfast in the love of God, we can stand the test of time. Let me repeat that: You *can* stand the test of time. Sometimes, we get so involved in loving ourselves that we forget about loving the people we should be loving. I am a witness that if you just love with the love of God, He will do awesome things in your life and in the lives of those you touch. I never considered myself a "fuzzy wuzzy" kind of loving person. But when I love, I know that I love deeply, I am committed, and my love does not waiver. Appropriately, I am what my name says I am – Ruth, a beautiful and faithful friend. But even the most faithful friend can get tired along the way. It's the love of God that keeps us steady.

God said to me, "*Ruth, forget about trying to be loving, and don't be fooled by people who come across as being naturally loving. What I need you to do is to be a vessel for me and allow me to put my love in you and to pass my love through you because you're my arms in the earth. Therefore, I need you to open up yourself and just allow me to pass my love through you. It's not about how you feel. It's about your expressing yourself to people the way I say you ought to express yourself."*

I thought to myself, *"That's easy, God."*

He said, *"Everything I do is easy. My yoke is easy, and my burdens are light. You are making it heavy because you're trying to do things in your own strength, and that is impossible to do. Just open your heart and let me love through you, and I tell you, that is easy."*

Why Is Love Important?

To find the answer to this question, let's look at a passage of scripture in the book of John:

> *As the Father loved me, so have I loved you: continue ye in my love. If ye keep my commandments, you shall abide in my love, even as I have kept my Father's commandments and abide in His love. These things have I spoken to you, that my joy might remain in you, and that your joy may be full. This is my commandment, that you love one another, as I have loved you. Greater love hath no man than this, that a man lay down his life for his friends. Ye are my friends if you do whatsoever I command you. Henceforth, I call you not servants; for the servant knoweth not what his lord doeth:*

3

> *but I have called you friends; for all things*
> *that I have heard of my Father I have made*
> *known unto you. Ye have not chosen me, but*
> *I have chosen you and ordained you that ye*
> *should go and bring forth fruit, and that*
> *your fruit should remain: that whatsoever ye*
> *shall ask of the Father in my name, He may*
> *give it you. These things I command you,*
> *that ye love one another.* (John 15:9-17)

Jesus Loves Us Like the Father Loves Him

John 15:9 says, "*As the Father hath loved me, so
have I loved you.*" Can you fathom how much and
how seriously and how wonderfully God the Father
has loved His Son Jesus Christ? And if you can
fathom it, can you believe Jesus has loved us the
same way? What a revelation this is! It's a perfect
love. God the Father loves Jesus so deeply, and by
His words, His deeds, and His sacrifice, Jesus lets
us know that He loves us just as much.

Those who follow Christ should never feel unloved.
If you are married, it doesn't really matter so much
as to how your husband loves you – good or bad –
as long as you understand that Christ loves you. The
love of Christ will turn you around and cause you to
interact with your spouse in a way that will draw
him or her back to you, even if your spouse is not
acting properly. Instead of getting caught up in how
your spouse is behaving, you need to get caught up

in God. Get caught up in the Word. Get caught up in Jesus Christ. Get caught up in the Holy Spirit, and then God himself will do the work on your heart and in your marriage.

At one point in my life, God revealed to me that I was off course emotionally, psychologically, and even spiritually because I relied so heavily on my late husband's love. He was a great husband. He looked after me. He basically took care of everything, and he made it easy for me. He liked to decide everything from what we would eat and where we would go. At first, my independence kept me from appreciating this, but when I finally made the transition to giving him control, I loved it.

I became accustomed to his taking care of me. When my husband's declining health rendered him incapable of handling some things, I had to stand up on my own two feet again. I realized quickly that just trying to decide what to eat every day was stressful. As independent as I used to think I was, the truth was that I needed someone else to take the reigns. It was difficult for me do it on my own.

In that hour, God said to me, "*I want you to get one revelation out of this entire experience if you don't get anything else: I want you to learn to lean on me and me alone. I don't want you to trust the arm of the flesh. I need you to get in me and get focused on me; stay in me, and the rest of your relationships in the natural world will be like icing on the cake. Your other relationships are like having dessert, but that is not what sustains you. I'm the one who sustains you. I am the main course – I am your God."*

Abide in the Love of Jesus

Because Jesus loves us with the same love that His Father has for Him, we should abide in His love according to John 15:9. But what does this really mean? To abide in love simply means to *stay in love* with Jesus. Do you know that you don't just automatically stay in love? Think of the most perfect marriage you know. Chances are, even that couple has to really work at staying in love, no matter how much they actually love each other. They have to hold hands. They have to say nice things to each other. They have to go out to dinners, sit across the table, look into each other's eyes and say kind words. They have to go back to the day they first met and be reminded how they felt that day. Relationships of any kind have to be nourished and nurtured. The fire does not stay lit just because you stay in the same house together. If you don't nurture your love, it will die, and the two of you will be left sitting there just looking at each other. It is the same in our relationship with God. It is important for us to nourish and nurture our relationship with Him.

Abiding in love means sharing with each other wherever you are and knowing that whatever you experience, that person is right there with you because they love you and you love them. To rekindle new feelings for an old love, it sometimes helps to change the scenery. I'll never forget a time when members of our family rented an RV and took a short trip. We weren't even sure where we were going, but we were going somewhere. It was going to be a change of scenery. We were all excited and enjoyed our time together with laughter and making memories. Sometimes you need to change the scenery, and you'll be surprised how much it will stimulate your relationship. Therefore, we have to abide in love. We have to remain in love. We have to consistently stay in the Word of God so that we will know how to nurture the love we have for God and others.

Keep God's Commandments

John 15:10 says, *"If ye keep my commandments, ye shall abide in my love; even as I kept my Father's commandments, and abide in His love."*

We must keep God's commandments and be obedient to His Word. God owes us nothing whether we are obedient or not. Instead, God loves us, and He provides for us because He loves us. However, just because He is a loving God is no excuse for taking Him or His love for granted.

A Word on Love

Agape love is not a free pass to do as we please. Obedience is the key that opens the door, allowing God to give us all that He has for us. Yes, He loves us in spite of everything, and He will forgive us, but there's a condition in the relationship that requires us to keep His commandments if we want to come into the fullness of that love.

Now, let me say quickly that the commandments that God has given us in His Word are definitely meant to be followed. Jesus came to fulfill the law – and that is the law of sacrifice! Before Christ, no man could stand without sin. Everyone fell short. As a human being, Jesus showed us that it was possible to follow the law. He gave up His deity and came to earth to show us how to live. He came willingly as the Father desired for Him to come, following His Father's commands just as we are instructed to do so.

Just as Jesus showed us by example, we simply have to follow the Father's commands also. We have to live according to the Word. Many people mistakenly view Christianity as a "*no*" way of life, with stringent rules and regulations. However, there is a distinct difference between rules and boundaries. God loves us so much that He gave us boundaries. This is indeed the mark of a good parent, for a child without boundaries is a child who is headed down the wrong path. God's rules are, in effect, yet another way He loves us, because He wants us to obey so that we come to no harm and stay on the right path. According to John15:10, we will abide in His love if we keep His commandments, so logically speaking, when we do not keep His commandments, we will be outside of His love. Yes, there are a lot of commandments, including the original ten. *"Thou shalt not have no other gods, thou shalt not make unto thee any graven image, thou shalt not take the name of the Lord thy God in vain, remember the Sabbath day, honour thy father and thy mother, thou shalt not kill, thou shalt not commit adultery, thou shalt not steal, thou shalt not bear false witness, and thou shalt not covet"* are all commandments from God. Taking care of our bodies as God's temples is also commanded, as is loving our neighbors.

Which one of these commandments can we abandon? **None!**

We must keep them all! We must hold them as high priorities because there are no standards where there are no rules. Boundaries are necessary because they help children understand where they are in their walk with their parents and with God.

John 15:10 states, *"Even as I have kept my Father's commandments, and abide in his love."*

Jesus could have chosen not to go to the cross, but because He loved His Father and because He was willing and wanted to abide in the love between Him and His Father, He had to follow the commandment of His Father by dying on the cross for our sins. Jesus had a choice to obey or not to obey; had He chosen disobedience, we would all be lost. He obeyed because He loved God and because He loved us.

So, if God loves us anyway and Jesus already paid the price for our sins, why should we obey? The answer is simple. You will always be loved by God, but you cannot be in love with God if you are not living in obedience. You cannot experience the joy and peace that comes with being in love if you are not following His commandments. You must understand that you cannot live any way you choose and still be able to abide in His love. Sin will keep you from staying in love. Don't have the misconception that sin is just about smoking, drinking, dipping, chewing, cursing, sleeping around, or other things that are visible.

Sometimes sin can occur when we are out of balance. I was in sin when I was out of balance emotionally, spiritually, and physically. Why? Because I was not obeying the Spirit of God when He was saying that I needed to take a break. Ignoring the Holy Spirit is just as much of a sin. My need to take a break did not happen suddenly. I ignored a lot of things that the Holy Spirit was saying to me before it happened, and every time I ignored His voice, I was in disobedience to what God was saying, and I paid the price. I eventually listened to the voice of God, and He restored me. God is a good God! I appreciate His correction as part of His total love. I appreciate His loving me enough to continue to speak to me until I came to a place of obedience.

John 15:11 says, *"These things have I spoken unto you, that My joy might remain in you..."*

The joy of the Lord is our strength. When the Lord's joy is your strength, you don't get weary. However, the Lord's joy does not remain in you if you're not keeping His commandments. In order to have that full joy in us, we have to remain in love with Jesus Christ. If Jesus' joy is in us, then we have the full strength. John 15:11 goes on to say, *"...and that your joy might be full."*

Can you just imagine the fullness of the joy of Jesus Christ? He has to be full of joy because He's done everything that God told Him to do. So Christ *IS* perfect joy, and those of us who let Him in and follow Him in obedience can live in perfect joy.

Love One Another

John 15:12 is a well-known passage that many people can recite from the time they are small:

A Word on Love

"This is my commandment, That ye love one another, as I have loved you."

Reciting this passage is meaningless unless we remember that Jesus is the ultimate, perfect example of love. We should love others like He loves us. The only way we will be able to do this is to allow God to love others *through* us. He will let you know what to say and what to do to show love to others.

If you don't love your brother who you look at every day, how can you love God whom you can't even see? It's not just about loving God either, but also the love that is in us that God would transcend and have manifested in our day-to-day walk with others.

Love manifests itself in our home relationships. While it is important to love your Pastor and other members of your church, it is contradictory and hypocritical if you then go home to your own spouse or your own children and have no love for them.

Love begins at home. Having a good attitude and showing kindness towards the people in your home starts a chain reaction, resulting in being kind to others. If you love your family, you will have a more perfect love towards the people in the kingdom of God. God knows us. He sees us. He knows how we're behaving at home. If you're married, love your spouse. If you have children, love your children. It is as simple as that.

Lay Down Your Life

John 15:13 reads, *"Greater love hath no man than this, that a man lay down his life for his friends."*

Do you know what is it to lay down your life for someone else? When children have strayed away from God and parents, keep praying and believing that these children are going to live for God again, that's what laying down your life is about. Even when you don't want to, you make up your mind to stand in the gap for another person – to help another person when they are in distress. Laying down your life is also saying yes to spiritual leadership. It's doing your best at whatever is asked of you in ministry. That's what it means to lay down your life.

Jesus is so wonderful because He has demonstrated His love to us by laying down His life on Calvary. But we can lay our lives down for others every day in countless ways by devoting ourselves to loving those around us and doing all we can, even sacrificially, to help them. All of the saints who are alive today, as well as those who have passed on before us and those who will be born again are the fruit of Jesus laying down His life for us.

Aren't you glad He laid down His life for you? Are you willing to lay down your life for someone so that they might come to know God in a more fruitful way? Are you willing to lay down your life so that you might encourage someone to hold on when they've lost faith? Anybody can give up, but only God can help us to stand. You can hold fast to laying down your life for someone so that they may come forth stronger. It's the best thing you can do… to be a friend. When Jesus became my friend, I was not worthy. Don't have the attitude of some who say, "*If you're worthy, I'll love you. If you're worthy, I'll do this for you. If you're worthy, I'll come with you. If you're worthy, I'll stay with you.*" That's not the way Jesus functions (and it's a good thing because none of us are truly worthy of His love), and that is not the way we're supposed to function either.

God Calls You "Friend"

Christ died for you when you were yet a sinner. You were an enemy of God, yet He gave himself for you. Jesus said in John 15:15, "*Henceforth I call you not servants; for the servant knoweth not what his lord doeth; but I have called you friends; for all things that I heard of my Father I have made known unto you.*"

You are now in the family, as if you've married and are now eagerly invited to the family meetings.

Jesus says, *"We're having a family meeting. Join us."* Therefore, as His people, we should welcome others to the family as openly. God calls us His "friends" even though we don't deserve it. We are not servants or sinners in God's eyes. We are His "friends," a part of His family.

God Chose You to Bear Fruit

You did not choose God; He chose you, according to John 15:16. When you choose something, you can say, *"I don't want it anymore."* You cannot give Christ back. God chose you. I'm so glad I can't give Jesus back. He chose me first.

He went on to say in John 15:16 that He *"ordained you; that ye should go and bring forth fruit, and that your fruit should remain: that whatsoever ye ask of the Father in my name, he may give it you."*

Christ chose us and then appointed us to go and bear fruit. Fruit of what? Fruit of love. Love produces everything. The Word says that even faith works by love. If you're not motivated by love, then your faith is fruitless because it is a self-serving faith. Fruit will remain, so whatever we do in Christ and in love, it will remain.

If you have something that is spoiling on the vine, check your love barometer. Find out what your fruit is founded on. If you say that it is founded on the

A Word on Love

love of God, it has to stand. The scripture says that whatever you ask of the Father in Jesus' name, He'll do it for you. Do you have any prayers that are held up? Check your love barometer. Find out how much you are really holding back from God and holding back from His people. God's Word says that you find worth in love with the Father, Son, and the people who God puts before you. If you aren't bearing fruit, you are not abiding in the love of God. You need to fertilize your crops with a healthy dose of God's love by staying close to God through obedience.

In this we have the victory. I challenge you today to walk in love. It is the most powerful grace there is. I'm so excited that God is refreshing my love – not that He's putting loveable people around me. Instead, He's putting around me people who challenge me to allow His love to flow through me. Are you finding it difficult to love? Will you stand for God and allow Him to love through you?

◆

2

--- ◆ ---

Just One Thing

Many of God's people get overwhelmed by all of the things they think they have to do. As a Pastor, I try to teach about various lessons and minister to so many needs, but often the messages go in one ear and out the other. Of course, this can be very frustrating. I often find myself just whining to God about it. I reached a point where I felt as if we would have to start teaching and laying the foundation all over again because we still need so much increase and strength in the body.

"How do we do that?" I questioned.

God answered me simply, *"There is only one thing you need to get straight, Ruth – just one thing! That thing is that you must love God with everything in you. Just this one thing will put everything in place."*

Just one thing! Isn't it just awesome to realize there is just one thing we have to get straight?

In Matthew 22, we read:

> *But when the Pharisees had heard that he had put the Sadducees to silence, they were gathered together. Then one of them, which was a lawyer, asked him a question, tempting him, and saying, Master, which is the great commandment in the law? Jesus said unto him, Thou shalt love the Lord thy God with all thy heart, and with all thy soul, and with all thy mind. This is the first and great commandment.* (Matthew 22:34-38)

Now we know we need to love God, but how do we do that? Maybe you say, *"I'm trying my best. I love Him the best I know how."*

First of all, we've got to understand who God is. If we don't know who people are, we won't know how we're supposed to love them. God is everything, the beginning and the end. He is the one constant in everything that has been and ever will be. Whether you want Him to be or not, He is there in every breath of your life and in every moment before and after it. He has the power to control everything around you. I cannot begin to try and define all that God is, but first of all I want you to know that God is self-existing.

Our Self-Existing God

Every one of us came forth from somewhere, but God is self-existing. The mere fact that He's self-existing lets us know that He's got something on us. You know the old adage "Respect your elders!" The reason this holds true is because you can learn a lot from the people who have already been to places you haven't been and crossed bridges you have not yet had to cross. If we know we can learn from our elders because they are older and wiser and have been around longer and been through more, then why would we not consider that God would be the wisest of all, considering that He was here before the beginning. He's not just older and wiser – He's the oldest and wisest because He has always existed.

John 5:26 tells us that *"the Father hath life in himself; so hath he given to the Son to have life in himself."* Therefore, both the Father and the Son are self-existing. Because they're self-existing, they are bigger and beyond anything we can imagine. Because they're beyond everything that's been created, we know that there's awesomeness in the Father and the Son. If you meet a young woman or young man and they try to talk to you, the first things you want to know are, "Who are you? What's your background? What are the things you used to do?" It's natural to question someone before you start to trust or love them, especially in a day and age where it is easy to be deceived into getting involved with the wrong people.

But the Father is self-existing. Colossians 1:17 talks about Jesus Christ and says that everything that's been formed was formed "*by him and for him*" and that everything "*consists through him.*" Does this not sound like someone worthy of loving? We can love Him and trust Him because He is a part of everything that is, was, and ever has been.

Our Immutable God

Not only is God self-existing, but He's also immutable. In other words, He cannot change. There is nothing about God that changes. He is consistent and constant. Wouldn't you just love to meet a few folks who are unchanging? Most of us know a few people who change with every breeze. But not God. He is unchanging, so you can trust what He says to be true today, tomorrow, and fifty years from now.

One of the things that I loved about my late husband was that he was dependable. A quality of consistency in someone is not necessarily always a good thing. If his ways annoy you, you will want them to change. But still, the main advantage with a person like that is that you always know how to approach him. That's why I admired this characteristic in my husband.

However, unchanging people can be difficult when life-shattering events happen, when the world rearranges right in front of them, and they don't seem to notice or adjust in any way, or they don't know how to handle the sudden changes. When my husband began to get sick, it was difficult for both of us.

God's unchanging ways, on the other hand, are always perfect. No matter what happens, God offers delivering power and restoration and enables those who love Him to be anointed and yield in those areas where it's needed.

Even though there are a few people who seem unchangeable, the truth is that people are always changing – sometimes for the better and sometimes for the worse. If you don't believe this about people, think about the yo-yo dieting cycle that so many people endure, including me. Over the years, I've admittedly put on a few extra curves. I've been disciplining myself and getting my body back into shape, trying to eat healthier. While these efforts are for a physical change, they also represent a truly revelational spiritual change.

The devil will try and fool you into thinking that some changes aren't that important, that they are material or physical and are not worth your efforts in the long run. But in my case, as I began to watch myself get in an unhealthy relationship with food, I said, *"Oh my God! What's going on here?"*

A Word on Love

Making any change can take everything within you. It's not just a matter of saying, *"Just discipline yourself."* In many cases of change, you need to pray and have people praying for you. You might even need to practice fasting, and keep yourself meditating on the Word. In the case of making physical and diet changes, you need those around you to understand that they can't flaunt their deep-fried goodies in front of you.

One time as my late husband and I were battling this fight, he told a waitress that he didn't want dessert, only to have her bring it back and give it to him for free. You don't think that was the enemy? If a change is worth making, chances are the devil will try and stop you, even if it involves cheesecake. But don't dismay because God is powerful! My husband brought that free dessert home and put it in the refrigerator, and by the time he even remembered it was there, it had gotten too old to eat! God will always be there to help you change if you need to. Always. Because He is immutable.

In the times that we're living in now, having an unchanging God is really important to me because people are changing. Things that I never thought would change are changing. Relationships are breaking down that I never thought would break down. People are making decisions right now that seem so obviously left-winged to me, yet they still think they are right. When right has become wrong and wrong has become right and we believe its truth, we have to remember that people's thinking can change. We also must remember that the devil is a liar, but God never changes his mind when it comes to righteousness.

Even when the people around us change their lives, their hearts, or their commitments, our God doesn't change and we should strive to be more like Him. We need to be like God, committed, and full of love.

What are love and relationships about? Commitment! Keeping covenant! We cannot tell someone we love them and then break covenant with them. Change in the form of growth can be good and certainly we are always changing in that sense. Love that begins with the love of God will not change because God's love is unchanging. Too many relationships have ended because the love is based on what people see for a moment. When that moment ends, they seek that moment somewhere else, leaving their commitments behind. This is a character issue. This is a heart issue. This is an internal issue. It's never external; it's always what's going on inside of a person.

So how do we keep from changing when we should hold tight to where we are? We have to make up our minds that we simply don't have a choice. Covenants are promises, and we have to keep them if we are striving to be like God, who doesn't break the promises He makes to us. He keeps them. Malachi 3:6 says, *"For I am the Lord, I change not..."*

Are you really striving to be like God, changing only to be conformed to His image? Are the changes you are choosing to make only the changes that you can find yourself in His Word? That should be the standard. We should never change unless the Word says so, and if the Word says we should change, we should do it.

We're still talking about love because the fact that God does not change is part of how He loves us. We can trust Him and know He will keep His promises, His commitments. That, my friends, is love. Hebrews 13:8 says Jesus Christ is *"the same yesterday, and today, and forever."* Are we His? Are we His body? Are we like Him? Are we obsessed with our own righteousness? We need to learn from God's self-existence, strive to be unchangeable and keep commitments like He does, and remember that He's also eternal.

Our Eternal God

The reason God's eternity makes a difference is because we, too, are eternal. We're going to live forever somewhere. We are eternal, so therefore, that's why we have to get our business straight. We need to realize that we need Jesus for this reason, to be born again.

We can't just live the way we want and arrive at heaven's gate by the seat of our pants. No, there's a responsibility that comes along with being a believer, a price to be paid. We've got to stand firm on what God says because God is eternal and He's going to live forever. He's going to exist forever, and He's going to be there on the day when we all stand as individuals to answer, *"What did you do, and how did you live?"* We are all going to have to give an account, one-by-one, for our own doings, and God loves us so much that He won't leave us in this condition.

Our Omniscient God

So, who is this God that we are supposed to love? Isaiah 40 talks about who God is:

> *Lift up your eyes on high, and behold who hath created these things, that bringeth out their host by number: he calleth them all by names by the greatness of his might, for that he is strong in power; not one faileth. Why sayest thou, O Jacob, and speakest, O Israel, My way is hid from the LORD, and my judgment is passed over from my God?* (Isaiah 40:26-27)

A Word on Love

Isaiah spoke here about the heavens and the stars and how they came to the beckoning call of God. Do you know how awesome that is? God can call the stars out and call them by their names. We may not know their names, but God knows their names, and He doesn't miss a single one.

If God is there and can name the stars, name by name, then why as human beings do we sometimes think our ways are hidden from God and that we can do whatever we choose to do? Our ways are not hidden from God. Thinking and pretending that our ways are right will not fool God. He will not overlook what we do, and we cannot hide it from Him. The everlasting God, the Lord, the Creator of the ends of the earth neither faints, nor is He weary. His understanding is unsearchable. He gives power to the weak and those who have no might, and He will increase their strength.

Are you feeling weak? Are you feeling like you don't have any strength? The Word of God says that God gives strength and power to those who are weak. Even youth shall faint and be weary, and even young men shall utterly fall. You can trust nothing in the flesh; your youthfulness will pass, but your God will not fail you. God will increase your strength when you need Him most.

I am over fifty now. Lord have mercy! I am more than half-a-century old! When I was in my twenties,

I thought my life was going to be so much longer and that I had so much life ahead of me, but these years passed so quickly. Where did they go? We need to grow older gracefully, and not get disappointed and disgusted with life. We should embrace every new place. I'm in the best part of my life right now. I'm enjoying this moment right now. Whatever this time is offering me, I'm embracing it with everything that is within me. I'm enjoying life today! I don't want to be twenty-five again. I want to be sixty, seventy, and so on, until God calls me home! God is so awesome because He gives strength when we can't rely on our youthfulness.

God said in Isaiah 40:31, *"But they that wait upon the LORD shall renew their strength; they shall mount up with wings as eagles; they shall run, and not be weary; and they shall walk, and not faint."*

That's the testimony that we as believers have if we hold fast and love God with all our hearts and mind and strength. What is our heart? That is the inner part, the depths of what we feel and everything within us. It's our minds, our intellect, and our thinking.

If you keep your mind on something, you'll increase your desire for it. You know how affairs get started? We meet somebody, and then we encounter them again, and then we start meditating on them. Whatever you meditate on will manifest

27

itself in your life. You know how to stop an affair? Stop meditating on it! Stop keeping your mind on it and you will lose your desire for it.

That's how it works; it's not complicated. When we fall into sin and we won't change our minds, guess what we have decided? We have foolishly thought, *"The Lord will ignore my doings. The Lord will let me get away with this."* I'm here to tell you that we must get just one thing right: **We must love God with all our hearts.**

There is no way to love God with all our hearts and then say that we can do whatever we want to do. That's not the way to do it. The reason people don't like to come to the altar and get on their face and spend time in the presence of God is because they don't want Him to show them their sin. As long as they stay in the outer-courts, they don't have to deal with it. But if you get in His presence, He will reveal to you what is really going on in your life. When He reveals it, you have to do something about it.

The most important thing we've got to get straight is that we need to love God first. Too many of us are *trying* to love people, and don't love God. That's why we can treat people any kind of way, because the love we have is carnal. But when the love we have is settled in God and the foundation is God, we will treat people the way God wants us to treat them. God will honor that love and that grace, but we have to love Him first and foremost. We cannot ignore God's love for us, and we have to love Him back.

◆

A Word on Love

3

Loving Yourself God's Way (Part 1)

Now that you know what love is and how to love God – who is love – I would like to share the importance of loving yourself God's way. In the next three chapters, I will deal with how our personality, feelings, and character affect who we are and how we love ourselves. Let's read a passage from Matthew 22:

> *But when the Pharisees heard that He had put the Sadducees to silence, they gathered together. Then one of them, which was a lawyer, asked him a question, testing him, and saying, Master, which is the great commandment in the law? Jesus said unto him, You shall love the Lord thy God with all thy heart, with all thy soul, and with all thy mind. This is the first and great commandment. And the second is like unto it: You shall love thy neighbor as thyself. On these two commandments hang all the law and the prophets.* (Matthew 22:34-40)

A Word on Love

Let's revisit verse 39 for a moment: *"And the second is like it: Thou shall love thy neighbor as thyself."* As I started thinking about this subject and prepared to teach on loving your neighbor, something dawned on me: the more I meditated on loving your neighbor as yourself and started digging into the loving yourself part, I got stuck. I realized that one of our big problems is that a lot of us don't love ourselves. A lot of us have a totally unhealthy love for ourselves, so it's not really any surprise that what we pan out to other people is not appropriate. If we are loving others the way we love ourselves, and we don't love ourselves correctly. Well, you see the problem. How do we love ourselves? How should we love ourselves? Our personality, which is shaped by many things including our culture, our looks, our self-esteem and our financial status, can affect how we view and love ourselves.

Our Culture

The first thing that influences and impacts us is the culture in which we were conceived. What I mean is, if we were born in a covenant loving relationship, we may be a little more balanced in our emotions and psyche and feel more secure in who we are. Many of us are born outside of covenant and outside of love, so we definitely may have some type of emotional wounds within our spirits that manifest in our day-to-day functioning.

This doesn't mean we're accidents. Only God gives life, and all of us, no matter the circumstance of our birth, are made in the image of God. But it does mean that there are dynamics within our personalities that are embedded through the culture from which we were conceived. If we're conceived in covenant and that covenant gets broken in the formative years of our lives, it could leave us feeling a little disappointed or rejected. As children, we cannot possibly understand what is going on with the adults, so we naturally blame ourselves. When we are young, we sometimes internalize what goes on in our culture. Basically, even the way our parents communicate and respond to us as young people can make a difference in how we see ourselves and how we function as we deal with the issues of life.

Not only do parents have a great impact on how we view ourselves, sibling rivalry can also be a real bugger bear! The jesting, joking, name-calling, and putting down that goes on between siblings has a much higher impact on the hearts and spirits of children than people realize. The children who suffer these things often grow up to be adults who have many broken places that have to be addressed.

Sometimes, our negative view of ourselves can stem from something in the culture that doesn't seem that serious. Simple things, like growing up in the culture that I grew up in, where being light skinned was good and being dark skinned wasn't so good. Long hair was good; short hair wasn't good. Nappy hair wasn't good; straight hair was good. It took a long time to learn it, because of the culture, but I'm so glad that we got it straight and that now we're black and we're proud.

I grew up in the era of the sixties, and I was a radical for my times. The reason I'm radical is because my Lord and Savior is radical. Radical simply means that you don't accept the *status quo*, that you want to change *status quo*. You want to set a new course of action. You want to make a difference. You're willing to put your life on the line to see some change, as long as it's going to change for the betterment of the future.

I had to understand the culture, growing up in the sixties and experiencing integration. I didn't know why White people didn't like me. I wasn't around them; I was only around Black people. I loved them, and they loved me back. So, to be thrown into a school system where I was now being called names and spat on and hit made me a fighter at school. You shouldn't have to fight at school, but those things get into your spirit, and they cause you to be all that you are. Those dynamics formulate who you become. Sometimes having a fighting spirit helps you to love yourself and teaches you to stand up for yourself so that you can love and stand up for others.

None of us arrived in the world in perfect form. Even if we're born in the best of circumstances, when we traveled from the womb of our mother and left that nice incubated place to enter this cold world, and the doctor popped us on our backside and cut our umbilical cord, we felt some rejection first thing. So if you thought you never felt rejection, I just want you to know that none of us arrived without some form of rejection.

Change causes us to feel the difference, and that is the temperament of rejection. So, we start our lives with instant rejection and have to live through cultural happenings in our homes and our societies that affect us in ways that make loving ourselves or others difficult. So, how do we love ourselves?

Let me tell you just a little bit about what God says about how we ought to love ourselves. First of all, Philippians 4:13 says, *"I can do all things through Christ which strengtheneth me."* Now that's the first order of business when learning how to love yourself God's way. Understand that you do not really have any disabilities. You can do anything that God purposes for you to do through Christ who gives us strength.

Here is an affirmation, which I want you to recite: *"Lord, never will I confess ever again that I am a failure because I'm not a failure. I can do all things through Christ who strengthens me."*

35

Repeat this over and over until you believe it and practice it. Praise God! You can do it. You can make it. Yes, we go through trials. Yes, we go through temptation. Yes, we get pressed down, but the Word tells us that we are not perplexed and we're not put down forever; we come back in Jesus' name. You can do it. It doesn't matter what the status you are in right now. It doesn't matter what you're going through right now. You must know in your own mind that because Jesus said it, you can do what you need to do. Remember that God never lies! We all need to have confidence and stop going back and forth in our minds as to whether we can or can't, whether we will or won't. You can do everything God says you can to do by His help, and you're not doing it by yourself. What a joy it is that we're not on our own! We know that we serve an unchangeable God. He's a self-sustaining God, and He helps us with what we need!

Our Financial Status

Philippians 4:19 says, *"But my God shall supply all your need according to his riches in glory by Christ Jesus."* Do you look at your checkbook when you start thinking about your needs? It's important, yes, but we must also remember that we also need to check our accounts in heaven.

Always remember, we need to look up to God, because the Word tells us that God is the one who

36

supplies all of our needs. He is the one who takes care of us. It's a faith walk. It does not matter how much you have or how much you earn. God will pass through our hands what we need, and on top of that, He will often bless us enough so that we can pass our riches on to someone else. God's blessings are often not just for us, they are given to us so that we can share them with others who need them. God supplies, and He supplies through people. The only reason it feels like a shortage is because God is putting stuff in our hands, and instead of us passing it on, we're putting it in the can, putting the lid on the can, and sitting on the can. God shows us His love by giving, and we need to pay that love forward whenever we can.

Money that is stagnant is not any good; money has to keep moving. Sticking a wad of money under your mattress accomplishes nothing but keeping you from a good night's sleep. Moving money is powerful. Find somebody to give something to, and keep it moving! If you have a dollar, share it; because God says that He is the one that supplies all your needs, and if you can participate in letting God be a channel through you, when you have a need, you'll have faith that God will use somebody else to be a channel for you. Amen!

Sometimes, loving yourself the right way means making efforts to fulfill your dreams. I want to appear on television. I keep saying it because I want to do this. I believe God put this dream in my heart. I need to make efforts to realize my dream even when it looks as though it may not be easy. I know, according to my favorite scripture, which is found in Romans 8:28, that*"...we know that all things work together for good to them that love God, to them who are the called according to his purpose."* I really love that Scripture, and I stand on it. Sometimes God shows me what's not His will when I run into a little restriction, but this doesn't mean we don't try. We need to press in and see what God says. If you have a dream that you believe God has given you, God is going to bring the resources you need, and it's not going to be an impossible struggle to achieve it.

But we have to make sure that we understand it is God who meets those needs and because of this, we can confess: *"I will never confess lack again!"*
So how do you address it when you feel like you've got urgent needs? You say, *"My God will supply all my needs according to His riches in glory through Christ Jesus."*

That's right, just confess the Word. Too many of us keep confessing the negative, confessing our circumstances instead of confessing what the Word of God says. This is who we are as children of God. This is how we love ourselves. Not loving ourselves comes from feeling like we've been done wrong, as if God hasn't come through for us. We may have been treated poorly from others in our lives from the beginning, but God is faithful to meet our needs and heal our wounds.

Our Confidence

Having confidence in your abilities and in God's faithfulness to provide are key to loving yourself. But we often feel we are lacking, like we can't accomplish our goals and dreams. That's why I want you to know who you are as God sees you. II Timothy 1:7 says, *"For God hath not given us a spirit of fear, but of power, and of love, and of a sound mind."*

So when the enemy tries to come in and say, *"You're losing your mind. You're not good enough. You will never succeed,"* you say, *"God has not given me a spirit of fear but of power and love and a sound mind."* Hallelujah! You begin to confess what the Word says.

Our confession is that we refuse to submit to fear. Simply say, *"I refuse to submit to fear,"* and say it with an attitude. Say, *"I will not fear anything! Fear of poor health? NO! I refuse to submit to fear! I refuse to submit to the idea that I'm going to be homeless. I refuse to submit to the idea I'm not going to have enough to take care of my family. I refuse to submit to that fear."*

A Word on Love

Whenever there is fear, there is lack of faith. The Bible says only faith pleases God. This is who you are. This is what you already possess in Christ. Just being in Christ Jesus is your inheritance as a child of God. You don't have to do anything to receive this privilege. Jesus gave the inheritance to you when you accepted Him. All you have to do now is work it out and claim what is yours. I'm excited about this Word, because it is blessing my life just to learn who I am and to love myself more like God loves me.

Our Physical Bodies

Loving ourselves is not about looks, either. It's not about the size of our bodies. It's not about how tall we are or what color we are. It's about knowing who we are in God. Too many of us spend too much time measuring ourselves against other people physically. But the reality of it is we are people of God. We're created in God's image. According to a verse in Psalms, we are *"fearfully and wonderfully made,"* and that means ALL of us! He didn't say *"a few of us are fearfully and wonderfully made."* We don't have any reason to do anything but to rejoice.

Psalms 27:1 says *"The Lord is the strength of my life."* Do you feel weak in your body? Do you feel weak in your mind? Do you feel weak in any way? The Lord is the strength of your life. It's not you. You don't have to have the energy in yourself. You have to know that it's the Lord that is the strength of your life. Do you feel as though you can run a race if you know the Lord is your strength? Oh yes, that's how we do it.

People say all the time, *"Pastor, how do you do it?"* I just keep going, going, and going. The Lord is my strength. It's not our natural strength. It's the Lord that gives us strength to do what He says to do. Our confession is this, *"I will not assume weaknesses or frailty."* These bodies are not who we really are – we are spirits who live in a physical body.

I lived in Greensboro, Alabama and grew up in a house where you could look through the floors and see the ground. I could almost look up and see the sky. But that didn't determine who I was. From there, I've traveled around the world. Just because your house is a little raggedy, it doesn't mean there's anything wrong with you. Just because the body is a little frail, it doesn't mean that something is wrong with you, because you're not your body. You are a spirit, and God loves you in the spirit. He loves your spirit, and you should love your spirit.

That's why the Word of God says in Ecclesiastes 9:11, *"...the race is not to the swift, nor the battle to the strong...."* It also says in Zechariah 4:6 that it's *"...not by might, nor by power, but by my spirit, saith the LORD of hosts."*

41

A Word on Love

Once you put your mind on the things of God, you are somebody to be reckoned with; you are part of a mighty people. You are somebody special in God, and you ought to love yourself. You are accepted in the beloved. Nothing that comes against you will prosper, so you don't have to be afraid of anything. Fear God and Him alone because He's the one who can do something and make the difference.

How you feel is important, but don't let how you feel about the cares of this world – money, appearance, atmosphere, etc. – determine whether or how you love yourself. Love yourself in spite of how you feel and you will be in a better position to love others through the awesome power of God.

4

·◆·

Loving Yourself God's Way (Part 2)

How we feel affects how we love ourselves. Most of us have different types of defense mechanisms. If we're attentive, we can recognize them in our interactions with people. If we're not aware of them, we may respond without even thinking about what's going on around us. Sometimes we can tell what's going on with people even if they're not really trying to reveal themselves to us. I will discuss four specific types of defense mechanisms and then I will share scriptures that help us to allow God to be our defense. The Word is powerful and can help us fight through and survive any circumstance.

Denial

One thing we do as a defense mechanism is that we live in denial. Denial is to refuse to acknowledge or perceive that which is threatening or unpleasant. This is often done through escapist activity. My late husband was a professional at escapist activity. When he didn't want to hear what I was saying, he would log on and begin to work on his computer.

A Word on Love

When I attempted to talk to him and he wasn't really interested in what I had to say, he would select a game on the computer and begin to play. I really didn't mind this behavior as long as he didn't leave the room. I was aware that if I put the information in the atmosphere, even if he wasn't paying total attention to me, he was going to hear some of it.

Mind you, most of the time what I was talking about was not life and death stuff, just stuff that I wanted to talk about. I'd say, *"Honey, let me tell you this,"* and he could tell it was one of those times that I wanted to talk more than he wanted to listen. So he just escaped into his game. If you are married, you may be having trouble with a spouse who is escaping. You might not admit they escape, but that's my point. Whether we admit it or not, there are times when we all try to escape.

I also need to escape. When my late husband told me the story about his childhood and how he met someone very influential who helped to steer him in the right direction – a story I heard for twenty-five years straight at least once a day – I said, *"Okay, honey, I need to go make the bed,"* or *"I need to go to the kitchen,"* or *"Don't you want some water? Let me get something for you."* I was trying to escape. We're all escapists. We live with people who attempt to escape from us from time-to-time. It's healthy to escape once in a while because sometimes a little escaping action keeps peace. It made things more peaceful in my house because my husband wasn't getting frustrated with me trying to talk when he didn't want to talk. Oftentimes, being able to escape is a blessing in disguise.

Projection

Not only do we live in denial at times, we also project. Projection is placing blame for unpleasant or harmful realities upon someone else other than self. Have you ever met people who claimed, no matter what was going on with them, it was someone else's fault? They could do no wrong, and no one else can do anything right. This type of unloving feeling is called projection, and it's a type of defense mechanism. It may be that a person who projects constantly grew up being held accountable for a lot of stuff that might not have been their responsibility or criticized for stuff that they really didn't do. So, they learned to escape from being responsible by turning the tables and figuring out how to make somebody else be responsible, and the pattern doesn't just quit when they grow up, nor does it just quit because you get saved.

Rationalization

A third defense mechanism is rationalization, the excusing of one's unacceptable behavior by outlining its logical, rational virtues. People who rationalize often know what they're doing is not responsible thinking; however, they find a way to explain their behavior with logic and reasoning. In our heart of hearts, we generally know when we are doing something wrong, but we begin to rationalize to a point where we can accept our actions without feeling bad about them.

Fantasizing

Fantasizing is another means of escaping a reality we do not want to face. It happens when we try to fulfill frustrated desires by erecting an imaginary world as we would like it to be. Are you living in a fantasy world? While it may seem like fun and games to imagine your own private utopia, when it crashes, the crash is hard.

Because we need to know ourselves before we can love ourselves, and we need to love ourselves before we can love others, understanding the ways we try to escape from uneasy situations and defend ourselves can help to develop better and healthier relationships – with ourselves, with God, and with others.

When I was first married, my husband talked about how wonderful I was and what a perfect wife I was and how he just loved me with all his heart. He never mentioned any of my lesser qualities and would only talk about how wonderful I was. While most wives would enjoy this, I noticed a problem with it. I thought, "*If he can only love me if I'm perfect, one day he's going to get tired of me because I'm surely not perfect.*"

So I started asking him, "*What is it that you would like for me to change? What is it that you would like me to work on?*"

He said, "*Nothing. You're perfect. You're great. I love you. I'm fine with the way you are. Whatever you do is all right with me.*"

This went on for four or five years before one year I asked him that question again. I said, "*Honey, what is it that you want me to work on? I know that I frustrate you sometimes, because sometimes even though I love you, you frustrate me also.*"

He answered, "*Yes, there are some things I would like for you to work on. Let me tell you what they are...*" And he went back before Jesus was a baby and came all the way up to the moment in time! By the time he was finished, I was in tears.

To be honest, I was hysterical. What made me upset was the fact that all these years he lived with me unhappy about so many things and would never tell me. Then, after much prodding from me, he let me have it all in one shot!

A Word on Love

I said to myself, "*I knew I wasn't perfect, so if you told me this a little bit at a time, I could have handled it, but now all this, that, and the other all at once! Oh, I don't like this at all.*"

Well, you know what I did? I went into a state of projection. I said, "*It's your fault because I've been asking you for five years, and you haven't told me, so it's not my fault I'm not a good wife. I'm good like I am, because I'm not changing. I've been doing things this way too long now.*"

You have to recognize when escapism, projecting, rationalizing and fantasizing are taking place in your life in order to understand your mind and emotions. If you are not aware of these defense mechanisms, you will continue to do these things, believing that they are just your *personality*. Instead, these are defense mechanisms that you build up to protect yourselves. Defending ourselves may provide some sense of temporary comfort, but the only way to deal with our feelings properly is through the Word of God.

I was motivated to begin training in the field of counseling because of my love for people; I wanted to help them use the Word to get through difficult situations. I saw far too many hurting people, and I would preach to them and lay hands on them, and then they would leave. But often as they walked out, I would see their faces and realize that there was more that needed to be unlocked in their minds and emotions that didn't happen at that moment. I began to study so that I could gain professional knowledge so that I could help people more. Surprisingly, I had no idea that God wanted to help me in the process; however, His master plan was to make me healthy and to make me whole. Therefore, what I learned has helped me more than I've helped others, and I thank God today because it helped me to understand not only others, but also myself.

Now, as we love ourselves God's way, no matter how we have been affected and no matter how we handle relationships, we begin to understand ourselves the way God sees us, and we begin to fill our minds with new thought processes that push aside old thinking. That's why it's so important to continually get the Word in you, because you cannot be full of the Word and full of negative unrighteous thinking. Sometimes simply putting the Word on something we can't cast out will force it out of our hearts and minds, and the next thing you know, you'll be rejuvenated with positive thoughts and actions.

God Is Greater than This World

The first thing we want to understand is that according to 1 John 4:4, when we love ourselves God's way, we never succumb to circumstances of life because we know that *"...greater is he that is in you, than he that is in the world."* It doesn't matter what the world throws at us since we know that the God that is in us is greater than this world.

We recently funeralized the brother of one of our Elders. I had the opportunity to be by his bedside hours before he passed away. It is difficult to see someone who is in the state where they are trying to communicate with you while their body is sending a message that the end is near. Sometimes when you are at the bedside of someone who is dying, your faith wants to go here and your mind wants to go there. *"What do I say, Lord?"* I thought. I simply said to the person, *"I love you and care about you, and I'm praying for you, and I'm here."* He passed away within two hours from that time.

But the Lord said, *"Talk to the family. Their loved one is fine and I have got him. I want you to gather the family and talk to them."* So, I went and talked to the family and helped to prepare them as much as possible. The exact things that the Holy Spirit said to share with them were the exact decisions and choices they had to make.

Each one of them said, *"Pastor, it was so much easier since you verbalized to us how to think and how to process through the decisions that we had to make."*

God is so faithful to us. Even when we're at that door of death, we don't have to succumb to anything because to be absent from this body in Christ Jesus is to be present with the Lord. The Elder's brother didn't succumb to anything; he simply made a transition to go from this world to be in the presence of His Father. So you don't have to succumb and be afraid of anything. Just live your life! Don't live to die – just live! Just live! Many of us spend too much energy on trying not "to do stuff" when we ought to just do what God says to do.

God Always Causes You to Triumph

Secondly, when you love yourself God's way, you never bow down to defeat because you know that according to II Corinthians 2:14, *"God...always causeth us to triumph in Christ."* In Christ, there is no defeat. Even when things look like they won't work out the way you want them to work, you'll find out that God is at work doing exactly what He wants to do. All we have to do is embrace God. We should not be afraid to seek and embrace God. Don't try to hold on to what God is obviously changing. Just embrace Him. I'm telling you, the victory is embracing God, not in the natural world, and not in what you can see, but in what God does. If you embrace Him, you'll have the victory.

A Word on Love

The home-going service for the Elder's brother was on a Friday, but the day after he passed, I went by to see the family at the house. I met a young woman who was upset because she was a friend of his and she was also ill. The two would often venture to the doctor together and she felt a great loss when he passed away. In talking with her, I discovered that she was already saved but unchurched, and the one thing that the deceased brother had done was to try to get her to visit his church.

I said, *"So you'll be there for the home-going, right?"*

She said, *"Yes."*

I said, *"What a memorial it would be if you would just come and be a part of this family that he loved so much."*

She said, *"You know what, Pastor? I want to do that because you have really helped me today."* She came on Friday and joined the church.

Even when you feel defeated, God is always at work giving victory. You just have to look for the victory. Most of us get too focused on that which is negative. Rearrange your thinking. Decide from this day forward: *"I'm going to focus on the positive events that are going on around me. I'm not going to deny the negative; however, I'm going to put these events in their right place. I know that in Christ I am victorious, because God causes me to triumph always in Christ Jesus.*"

When we love ourselves God's way, we should refrain from claiming sickness. Additionally, we should not elevate sickness through excessive words, nor should we claim it as ours. You should never hear yourself saying "*my*" this or "*my*" that where it relates to disease. We should never parade sickness. I don't care what the ailment is. We should never promote sickness because the Bible tells us in Matthew 8:17, Jesus *"Himself took our infirmities, and bare our sicknesses."* He's already borne them, so when we talk about "*my*" this, that, or the other, we deny the power of what Jesus has done for us.

We have to be very careful how we speak about what's going on with our bodies. We cannot deny that our bodies will break down and become ill, but what we can do is say, *"The doctor says this, but I know this. The doctor says this, but I believe this. The doctor says this, but I'm healed by the stripes of Jesus."* You may acknowledge what the physician says, but then you put a "*but*" right in the middle of it because the "*but*" changes everything.

*"The doctor says that if my body has its way, I may not be here, **but God says** that I shall live and not die. I shall live and declare the salvation of the*

53

Lord. By the stripes of Jesus, I am healed, set free, and delivered." Hallelujah! This is the way we think and speak when we love ourselves God's way. Finally, this is the way we begin to see things.

God Cares for You

According to I Peter 5:7, we shouldn't worry. It says *"casting all your care upon him; for he careth for you."* Are you worried about something? How are the bills going to get paid? What is the report going to be when you get it? Are your children going to do what you want them to do? Are they going to make the progress you want them to make? Is your spouse going to do what you think they ought to do? According to the Word of God, we should cast all our cares upon Jesus, for He cares for us perfectly. Let me repeat that: He cares for you **perfectly.** Don't worry, because worry doesn't bring about progress. In fact, it only makes things worse by zapping your faith. Remember, don't worry, trust in God.

God's Peace Will Keep You

I am so thankful when I have an opportunity to live out the Word. Philippians 4:7 says, *"And the peace of God, which passeth all understanding, shall keep your hearts and minds through Christ Jesus."*

I was dealing with a situation where I answered a question at least fifteen times. Then, I was sent an email with five new options on it asking me to choose an option. I said, "*Lord Jesus, help me because if I answer this email, I am going to curse.*" I said, "*I don't need to curse, because you know if I say what I'm thinking right now, this is going to get forwarded all the way to Jesus!*"

Please remember that even if you don't send that email to God.com, He sees what we put in an email. We send all kind of foolishness to folks on email because it's easier to rant in a one-sided conversation without having to look someone in the face.

In this particular instance, I wanted to go "*nah, nah, nah,*" and I did. I said to myself, "*Okay, Ruth, back up.*" So I literally had to get up out of my chair and back up so I could help myself. I sent the message and said, "*Obviously we can't communicate, so I'm going to get somebody who I know can communicate with me to step in between us to handle this situation so that I can stay saved and continue to behave like I'm your Pastor. Thank you very much.*"

I am glad to report that I didn't curse and you will not read about this incident in the paper. Isn't love great? This is an example of real love! We're talking about love. This is why love is so important: Love keeps us from acting out.

We all have our issues – me included. If I had reacted to the email situation, it would have been an example of acting out, yet I was thankful that God checked me. He said, *"First of all, you don't have to deal with that situation. It is not necessary for you to address it at all. Just do this."*

I called one person. I said, *"I need you to do something for me."* And the answer? *"Yes, Pastor, no problem."* They took care of it, and I was so blessed and so thankful to see that when we let God handle things, we can have peace that passes understanding.

We do not have to act out our frustrations. Now, I used to say that showing frustration was a part of my personality; however, God taught me that this was an excuse. Specifically, showing frustration is *not* a personality trait. Frustration is the result of our belief that solving a problem in a Christian way takes too much time. We become impatient and our impatience leads to frustration. Instead of seeking peace, we go off on people!

Don't show frustration because the peace of God, which passes all understanding, keeps your hearts and minds in perfect peace. When you love yourself God's way, you look to God for your answers. You don't look to your flesh for answers, and if you stay in God, you will not react without thinking in a Godly manner.

God Ensures Our Freedom

Ensuring our freedom is an important part of loving self. II Corinthians 3:17 says, *"...where the spirit of the Lord is, there is liberty."* So those of us who love ourselves God's way will never allow anyone to put us in bondage – no one!

This can mean the obvious, but it can also mean that we should use our freedom to make the right choices when we have the opportunity. For instance, I recall a situation with my late husband in, which I began to want to project, to make him responsible for something that was my responsibility. When I opened my mouth, the Lord began to say something else out of my mouth. *"No, that's not what I'm trying to say, Lord. I'm trying to say that he should have handled this differently,"* I thought. But every time I started to say something, the Lord intervened, reminding me that instead of blaming my husband, I should have realized that I could have stepped up and did just what needed to be done. I had the liberty to step up. I kept trying to say, *"But you...,"* but the Lord just wouldn't let me say *"but"* anything.

What dawned on me was that there was a liberty that I had but wasn't willing to use it. So my bondage was not in what my husband's action was, but within my own mind.

Have you ever been in a service and you just felt like doing something that wasn't considered normal during the service such as screaming or running or coming up to the microphone or testifying or singing a different song or telling the choir "*Stop that song and sing another song!*" or telling the preacher to sit down?. I wanted to tell the preacher to sit down, I wanted to tell the choir to change their song, and I wanted to give them a new song, but I sat on my hands. How many of us have stayed in our seats when we had the full liberty to do something the Spirit was calling us to do?

The question that a Christian should ask is how much damage do we do to the body of Christ when we don't obey God? Oftentimes, during a church service, there will be someone who is just waiting for something to happen, and that one thing that God told you to do could have been exactly an event that would lead them to Christ. I heard someone tell a story once about a preacher who was ministering during a service, and the Lord told him to get down on his knees and crawl to the door and crawl back. Why? Because when the preacher obeyed God's command, someone in the service came to Jesus. He said, "*I told the Lord, 'I'll believe your God today if that preacher gets down on his knees and crawls to the door and crawls back.'"* The preacher obeyed, thank God, because for all we know, the person might never have gotten saved. I know that was a ridiculous thing to do perhaps, but if the Lord says to do it, do it!

So how do you know when God is telling you to take the liberty? One way to tell is because many times God's way makes us feel uncomfortable; we might think, *"I'm going to look so foolish,"* while the devil's way makes you think, *"Oh, I'm feeling very confident and I'm going to look so good!"* Why? It is because God is not trying to make a reputation based upon our own understanding. He desires for us to build a reputation through Him. Don't ever be limited by what you think your reputation should be. Allow God to have liberty in your life.

God Will Not Condemn You

The final word is that: *"There is therefore now no condemnation to them which are in Christ Jesus, who walk not after the flesh, but after the Spirit."* (Romans 8:1)

We should never condemn ourselves. Conviction? Yes! Anytime we are in the presence of God and sitting under the anointing and hearing the Word, the Holy Ghost will bring conviction in our hearts about those matters that we need to address. Accept the conviction, but don't view it as condemnation because they are not the same. Conviction is not meant to make you feel bad, instead it is meant to promote change and growth. Typically, we feel condemned because we do not want to change. Conviction will promote change and raise you to a higher level, rejoicing. This is when you claim the victory, and you'll be able to proclaim, "*I'm in a new place now. I'm more closely following that which God has called me to do.*"

◆

5

Loving Yourself God's Way (Part 3)

This question appears again. How do you love yourself God's way? We've already looked at loving yourself in spite of personality and feelings. Now, I'm going to talk about loving yourself in spite of your character. We're going to deal with character as it pertains to loving yourself God's way.

A noble goal of humanity is that we become and remain synergized. Webster denotes that synergy means being congruent. In other words, congruency denotes what we are the same inside and outside, the way we think is the way we behave, and the way we behave is the way we feel. Both our inner and outer selves should be as close to Christ-like as possible.

> *Jesus said unto him, Thou shalt love the Lord thy God with all thy heart, and with all they soul, and with all they mind. This is the first and great commandment. And the second is like unto it, Thou shalt love thy neighbor as thyself."* (Matthew 22:37-39)

A Word on Love

If we were the same inside and out, we would no longer have to use masks to cover up that which we don't want people to know about us. Rather, we would be able to live openly and honestly and allow people to see us exemplify Christ-like behavior.

Are you comfortable being yourself? When you're yourself, do people see a representative of Christ? A lot of us are comfortable being ourselves, but what do people see when they see us being ourselves? We need to be congruent. We need to make sure that we're one in the way we are functioning. So, in other words, our character will be the same as our personality and our feelings.

If our character and our feelings and personality are the same, then that means that every time a person sees us, every time a person talks to us, and every time a person deals with us, we remain the same. Don't you just love dealing with people who are consistent, especially if they are Christ-like? It just drives me crazy dealing with moody or wishy-washy people and never knowing how they are going to come off.

Do you know anyone like this? They have feelings and emotions that don't match up with their thoughts and their character, so what ends up coming out is mysterious behavior. You can fool people for a little while, but eventually our character is what we're going to live out. That's why it's so important that we love ourselves the way God loves us and according to the way He loves us. So let's look at the Scripture and a few things that God has said about how we should love ourselves and how our character should be.

I once said to one of my relatives, *"You know, faithfulness and commitment is my heart, my character. You know, that's my name...my name Ruth means 'faithful friend.'"*

He said, *"Oh, really? Is that right?"*

I said, *"Yes, as if you didn't know what my name means. Can't you tell this by my interactions with you?"*

My point is that you ought to be able to demonstrate what your character is just by the way you live your life, and that character should represent something godly.

According to Ephesians 2:10, we should never behave unworthy again. Why? Because we are God's *"workmanship, created in Christ Jesus unto good works..."* You are Christ's workmanship unto good works, so you don't have to ever feel unworthy. Wherever you are going, whatever you are getting, you deserve it. But I'm telling you, you're worthy not because of your doings, but because of what Christ has done and because of the love of God in you. You are worthy!

Be Content

Philippians 4:11 says, *"...for I have learned, in whatsoever state I am, therewith to be content."* Therefore, I choose not to display discontentment. When we love ourselves like God loves us, we will understand that although we may be in a tight place, God is at work in every situation causing it to work for our benefit and our good. For this reason, we don't have to be discontent and we don't have to express discontentment.

This is something I have to work on because I can often be discontent and whatever I feel, I tend to express. I'm so thankful for this because I realize His Word is true. God says that wherever we are, we can be content, and this is a part of character that should lead to action. God's love should direct our actions and these behaviors should reflect our love and obedience to God.

One way we can be content is to never let anyone intimidate or distract us from accomplishing our goals. Romans 8:31 says, *"If God be for us, who can be against us?"* For a few years now, I rearranged that text to say, *"If God is for us, who cares who's against us?"* We spend too much time wondering who's against us and who's for us and who's with us and who's not with us. This is a spirit of not knowing how much God loves you and not knowing how to love yourself like God loves you. When you love yourself like God loves you, sometimes you will feel like people love you even when they don't.

One of my biggest problems personally is that I often hurt people's feelings by saying something and assuming that I've been understood correctly. Do others come to you after you've had a conversation with them and tell you that you hurt their feelings? Maybe you're not as sensitive and don't get hurt yourself, so you have a tendency to speak more freely in your interactions with people. Remember, you have to make sure that you consider the other person's feelings. This is what God is teaching me. By the same token, we should try to remain objective so that we can really understand the heart of what people are saying. When you understand a person's heart and you see the intent of their message, then you go beyond the words to really understand the spirit of what they are communicating.

Even though we don't have to fret about who's against us, we still have an enemy. Yes, there is an adversary, and he is dangerously equipped with the power to deceive us. Yet as Christians, if we stay in Christ, the enemy has no power in our lives because of our status in Christ Jesus. However, if you're unaware of his devices, then he can overtake you. We want to make sure that you are aware that there are forces against us. Always know that we have the greater one in us and because of that, we can love ourselves the way God loves us.

Know that God Is Your Confidence

When it comes to loving ourselves the way God loves us, we cannot afford to be insecure. For some people, feeling self confident is very difficult. Proverbs 3:26 says, *"The LORD shall be thy confidence."* It is not I, nor my education, nor my upbringing, nor the color of my skin, nor to whom I'm married that is the source of my confidence! The Lord shall be my confidence and shall keep my foot from being taken. Who's going to do that? The Lord is going to do that. Because the Lord is going to do that, you can love yourself in spite of what is oppressing you or pushing against you, and you can love yourself the way God loves you.

God loves you so much that He says, *"I will be your confidence. I will be everything you need."* Are you feeling challenged about anything? If you're feeling challenged, I'm here to tell you that God is at work in that situation.

Think about what Jesus went through, about every step He took to Calvary. Would He still make that trip again today even after going through the pain and the suffering? Would He give up His life in this way all over again? YES! He would do it again because of what? He would give up His life because of you!

So many of us go through trials and tribulations and don't understand that God is at work doing a greater thing in us. There is a wise saying, *"When you go through trials and tribulations, God is getting you ready for a promotion."* So, the bigger your trial, the greater the promotion, if you pass the test and if you love yourself the way God loves you. It may not feel good to you physically or emotionally, but your spirit will know that this is God doing a new thing in your life.

We don't have to do anything except stand still and see the salvation of the Lord, because God loves us perfectly. He wants us to love ourselves the way He loves us. Good news! I will cease to fall under the troubles that come my way, and know that He is greater than all of my troubles combined.

Be of Good Cheer

So what do you do when troubles come? According to John 16:33, *"In this world, ye shall have tribulation: but be of good cheer; I have overcome the world."* Therefore, when trials and troubles press you, it's time to praise God! If you just give God praise, you get the victory in spite of what is going on. You can claim the victory no matter what the devil tries to say or what people say or what your body says or what your mind or emotions say. Additionally, you will claim the victory if you understand that God is at work in your life and that Jesus has already overcome, and since He has overcome and you're in Him, you have overcome also. Now, if you look at any situation you're facing right now and knew for sure that when you emerged on the other side, that it's going to be exactly what you desired, how different would you behave right now? Just think about it: you can see the other side of this matter, and you're there now, and you're looking back saying, *"Praise God! Thank you, Jesus. I am so glad that I went through this process. It did not feel good, and it was hard on me, but thank God I persevered and now the joy is set before me."*

Do you know that's the way God always does it? I cannot think of an experience that I've had (and I've had many) that I would not accept again. Yet, when I look at what God has done to me in the process – forget about *through* me – I would not take one experience back because if I did, I would not be what I am right now. Without these trials and tribulations, I would not be as strong as I am today. Trials and tribulations come to make us strong and come to test and prove the level of our faith. Additionally, they encourage us in the things of God, and they come to help us gain experience and this is all good. The Word works! I can stand here and teach you the Word of God day and night, but without the experiences He has brought me through, I would be hard-pressed to persuade you that God is able to do great deeds.

Learn How to Stand

I enjoy hearing the testimonies of people who have gone through trials and tribulations. Moreover, I enjoy hearing people that have a little experience under their belt, those who have tried the Word of God and found out that it works. It's all about faith. But faith and works ought to produce some results. If you have faith and you stand on the Word, you ought to see signs and wonders. Good things ought to be happening in your life. If I am frequently talking and teaching you something of God's good works, but you can't see any fruit coming from my life, what can I produce in your life? You can never give a person that which you don't possess. It doesn't matter how much you desire to give.

I would love to give you one million dollars right now, but it's not going to happen because I don't have a million dollars to give you. No matter how intense I may feel about it. No matter how much I want to do it. If I don't possess it, I can't pass it on to you or anyone else. This is similar to your life when you live in Christ. We need to learn how to keep loving ourselves the way God loves us. We move from our feelings and our personalities into our character into our actions into loving and performing what God has said in us and doing what He says to do. We've got to learn to walk this life out, and it's a day by day walk. It's a moment by moment walk. You receive salvation and enter a life-long process of living in a Christ-like way.

Now, I don't believe you get saved and then you can get unsaved. A lot of folk preach that, but I just don't believe it, and the reason I don't believe it is because of my experience. I may have fallen short of the glory of God, but I am still His child and I am still saved. If you have children, they are not going to stop being your children because they don't do what you ask of them. They may miss out on some benefits and blessings because of their actions, but they are still your children. The key is we have to go through situations and continue to grow in the process.

However, once you are saved, you enter into a process. That process requires you to stand up for Jesus in the good times as well as during bad times. You should stand up for Him whether you feel well or not, whether you look great or not, whether you exercise or not, whether you eat too much or not, and whether you are loving or not. It does not matter! Whatever your condition is, God is saying, *"I need you to stand, period."*

Recently, one of my dear friends said she had a client that owed her money, and the client said she was not going to pay her. My friend visited the client and said, *"I'm not here to argue. I'm just here to state my case, because it would serve no purpose for me to get excited and start flying off the handle."*

So the client said to her, *"I'm not going to pay you."*

My friend calmly took out the contract and set it on the table and said, *"It's in your contract that you have to pay me in this situation."* So they talked a little bit, and still the client continued to say she was not going to pay her debt.

My friend said that in that instant, she had a revelation not to touch the contract, but instead to let the client herself pick it up to find the information. So the woman finally reached over and picked up the contract, and as soon as she did that, it was over. Because whoever picked up the contract and moved first, they just lost. *"I guess I'll just have to pay you, won't I?"* she said to my friend.

What my friend knew was that getting all excited, throwing stuff, fussing, carrying on, and slandering someone lessens your credibility. A better strategy is to learn to manage yourself well. If you can't manage yourself well, you're probably not managing much else well either. When we face the devil and he says what we can't have and what we can't do, we've got to pick up our contract, and we don't have to even open it up and start yelling stuff at him because he already knows. We put it out there and say, *"That's our contract, and it says that I have a right to be right where I am. I have a right to have what I have. I have a right to have what I want. I have a right, I have a right, I have a right! My contract says it!"*

As long as you don't take a defensive position with the devil, you can win over him. But if you mess around and pick the contract up and start trying to beat him with it, you are going to lose that battle.

It is important for you to put your contact out there, because you know what it says, and so does the enemy. You know the conditions written in the contract and that contract was signed with precious, innocent blood, the blood of Jesus Christ! This blood will never lose its power! This blood cannot be erased! This blood that will never fade! This blood is still just as powerful today as it was the day that is was shed for our sins. We can continue to love ourselves because it's in our contract.

This contract is not just for leaders who are expected to stand, but it is for all Christians who should be ready to serve and carry out the plan of God. One day at a department meeting, I needed a Bible. I was the pastor and the preacher, yet I didn't even have a Bible with me. There were three or four deaconesses, and they didn't have a Bible either. There was a deacon, and he did not have a bible. One of the members, who does not have a title, said, *"Pastor, I have a Bible."*

I said, *"Yes, give it to me."*

She pulled out of her purse this dirty and mulled over little thing, put together with a rubber band and kept in a sack to keep from losing pages. She said, *"I have a contract!"*

I said to myself, *"She's an educator and does not have a spiritual title, yet she is an anointed woman of God, and she's very powerful in the Lord, but all of us were sitting there with titles, and we should have had our Bibles with us."*

None of us had one. You can't always tell a person's character just by looking at their title or by what they are supposed to be doing.

You've got to really get down into what people are about. I never would have imagined that this member carried a Bible. She said, *"I never leave home without it."* Now, I don't leave home without American Express, but you see the difference? Because of the call of God on our lives, we have a responsibility to minister, but the most power is not always in the pulpit. Sometimes, the most power is sitting in the pew where God's people are sitting. You have to be empowered to go forward and do what you can for the Kingdom. We have to love ourselves as God loves us, and in order to do that, we have to move from feelings and personality into character into action and into doing what God says and into living out His Word day-by-day. The more you do this, the more you'll feel God's love within you, and the more you'll desire to express and share love towards God. What happens is you will have perfect fellowship with God, and when you're in that perfect fellowship, you feel loved. When you feel loved, nothing moves you.

Part of having that fellowship with God involves making sure that your life is an open book and that your heart is right before Him. God gave me this simple principle recently. He reminded me that I don't repent enough. He said, *"You know you're forgiven, but you need to repent more. You need to confess your sin and faults more. In not doing so, you can begin to think that you don't have any."*

I said, *"You're kidding. I really do have some?"* I'm sure I'm not the only one who thinks like that. So now, each night before I lay down, included with my other prayers I pray a prayer of repentance. I confess my faults, my shortcomings, and my sins that I've committed throughout the day. Sometimes the Holy Spirit brings something specific to my spirit, and sometimes He doesn't. Even when He doesn't, I still repent for my sins that I know I've committed. Then, I get up in the morning and I fall on my knees again and I do a thanksgiving prayer, but I also do another repentance prayer.

I was telling this to a sister, and she asked, *"Why should you repent in the morning, Pastor? Is it a sin to sleep?"* I went on to explain that if you are married and your husband reaches over to touch you and you say, *"Honey, I'm sleepy,"* you should repent because you should have been available to him. That's the Word. Wives should be available. You can be tired, but you should be available. If you don't make yourself available, then you should simply repent. When we start to recognize sins that many people wouldn't even see, that is something to rejoice about because the Holy Spirit is working! If what I teach is not going to help you, then I may as well stop teaching. This is real teaching for real people who are in real situations that require some real Word – the Word of God.

A Word on Love

6

Having Love for Thy Neighbor

We began by understanding that the one thing we must do *first* is to love God. We learned how to love ourselves God's way, despite our worst traits. We found out that in God, we're victorious people, perfect in His sight, because He sees us through the redemptive blood of Jesus. We do not have to be sin-conscious or self–conscious; we need to be God-conscious.

This was all good news for me...safe, abiding, everlasting love for me and for you!

We also know that we need to love the pastorage and the visionaries who are working to help us carry out the plans of the Lord. We saw that we need to love our spouses and families.

In this final chapter, we will turn to the question of loving our neighbors. We'll begin by examining Exodus 11:

> *And the LORD said unto Moses, Yet will I bring one plague more upon Pharaoh, and upon Egypt; afterwards he will let you go hence: when he shall let you go, he shall surely thrust you out hence altogether. Speak now in the ears of the people, and let every man borrow of his neighbor, and every woman of her neighbor, jewels of silver and jewels of gold. And the LORD gave the people favour in the sight of the Egyptians. Moreover the man Moses was very great in the land of Egypt, in the sight of Pharaoh's servants, and in the sight of the people.* (Exodus 11:1-3)

God Can Make Your Enemy Your Provision

Often, we get frustrated with a neighbor who is really an agitator, that neighbor that we consider not to be the kind of person we really want to befriend. We think of them as enemies because we don't really wish to deal with them.

Every situation holds good news for the people of God. It doesn't matter what is going on, we can always find hope and life in the Word of God. In the above text the children of Israel were in bondage in Egypt, and Pharaoh was refusing to let the people go, although Moses had been before him according to what the Lord said, many times. The Lord tells Moses that Pharaoh is going to let them go – all of them. Then God does something interesting. He instructs Moses to have the people ask the Egyptians for their valuables. Egypt had prospered through enslaving the people of Israel. When it's time for God to make things right, He'll not only free you from your enemy's hand, but He will also recover your provisions from your enemy. God can be trusted to make things right again, so when you face someone who creates a problem in your life, consider looking closer and seeing how God will use that person in your life.

I remember a community where we lived with an interesting neighbor who didn't seem to care too much about children. We had a whole house full of children. We always had a house full of other folks and *their* children as well. While these particular neighbors were nice enough people, they just acted strange toward the children. For example, if, while playing, a ball went into the neighbor's yard, the children had lost it permanently. The children could not go into their yard and get anything. If the neighbors were home, they would come out quickly and get the toy and take the item in the house. They wouldn't say anything; they would just take it. We were always re-buying balls and re-buying everything that went into their yard. If it went into their yard, it was a provision for them to keep.

This was a problem, but I learned a valuable lesson when we stopped regarding it as a problem. Those same neighbors became our personal community watchmen. They did it single-handedly. We didn't have to have a group of people to watch the neighborhood. They watched the neighborhood, and if anything went down at our house, we knew what went down because those same neighbors who would pick up the children's toys and not let them have them back were also excellent watch persons. So on one hand, the toys were lost, but on the other hand, our neighbors provided an invaluable service.

Neighbors are inescapably in our lives, they are close to us even when we do not care to have them nearby. They're either right in your presence temporarily, or they live with you, or you pass them. Neighbors are people you have contact with in your daily life. Neighbors are people with whom you cross paths. Take the mindset that you will pay attention to the ways in which their presence provides or you rather than paying attention to the ways in which they agitate or inconvenience you.

Everybody I meet provides something for me. Some of them encourage me. Some of them inspire me. Some of them make me pray. Some of them make me know how frail I am without God. Some of them cause me to look inside and check myself. But all of this is necessary. We all love the person that encourages us, but what about the person who challenges us to make sure that we're better, to make sure we improve, and to make sure we increase or to make sure we don't stay the same?

No longer regard your enemies or those you do not care to befriend as a hindrance in your life, but as your important provision. Let's look at Exodus 12:

> *And the children of Israel did according to the word of Moses; and they borrowed of the Egyptians jewels of silver, and jewels of gold, and raiment. And the LORD gave the people favour in the sight of the Egyptians, so that they lent unto them such things as they required.* (Exodus 12:35-36)

They plundered the Egyptians. In other words, when they left Egypt, they stripped them. They left the Egyptians with nothing. It wasn't the people's doing; it was God's doing. That idea didn't come from the people's minds. In other words, God was saying, *"When you leave, I want you to take from the Egyptians what the Egyptians have taken from you."*

"The kingdom of heaven suffereth violence, and the violent take it by force," according to Matthew 11:12. We, as kingdom people, need to understand that God intends for us to rule and reign. We need to step up to the plate and do what God asks us to do. Sometimes we take the backseat position, and we do not take any responsibility. That's why our

nation is in such pain. The Bible says in Proverbs 29:2, *"When the righteous are in authority, the people rejoice: but when the wicked beareth rule, the people mourn."* So we have to make sure that we're not backing away from what God has given us to do and to possess. He wants to bless His people. Yet, we need to accept responsibility.

Nowhere in Scripture does God say it is noble to not have anything. Do you know Jesus became poor that you may become rich? Not only in spirit did He become poor, but also in the natural world so He could actually produce prosperity in your life. Every time we live beneath our privilege, we make an open show of the Lord again. We have to posses what God has given us, and God will give us favor. Your neighbors and your enemies are part of God's provision for you and being open to these people and what they bring will enrich your lives as God intended.

Do Good Deeds for Neighbors Who Are Less Fortunate

Proverb 3:27-28 says *"Withhold not good from them to whom it is due, when it is in the power of thine hand to do it. Say not unto thy neighbor, Go and come again, and tomorrow I will give; when thou hast it by thee."* What we have to do for the neighbor, if the neighbor is truly poor, is make sure that we are ready to give to that person. Now there's a difference between giving to someone and making provision for them. This is a person who came and asked something of you, and you're going to give that to them. It's an incident, a one-time situation, which can happen periodically. It's like growing up in the country.

I came from the country, and one of my Aunties lived down the street from us. It was my Mother's aunt, actually, and Auntie was well-to-do. So if Mother ran out of something, she would say, *"Take this cup and go down to Auntie and tell her to send me a cup of sugar."* We would go to Auntie's house and say, *"Momma said send her a cup of sugar,"* and Auntie would give her the cup of sugar. Momma would say, *"Tell her I'll send it back when I go to the store on Saturday."* Auntie said the same thing every time, *"Tell her that's all right."*

Mother never sent any sugar back to Auntie, no matter how many times I went down there to *"borrow"* it. If your neighbor is asking of you and you have it, it's a no-brainer, just give it to them. If you don't have it, you don't have to get all huffed up because you don't have it. Sometimes we go on a guilt trip because people ask us for something we can't provide, and then we feel condemned because we can't provide it, but if you don't have it say, *"I'm sorry, I don't have it. I'm out too."*

A Word on Love

We would sometimes go down to Auntie's house and she'd say, *"I'm sorry, baby. Please tell her I'm out myself, but tell her if your Daddy goes to the store, have him pick up a sack for me also."* And when Daddy brought her that sack of sugar, he wasn't about to charge her for it because she had favored us all those times and not received anything in return. A neighbor who lives next to you like that creates such a reciprocal relationship.

We were less fortunate than Auntie because Momma had so many kids. We just had more people to feed. It's just the truth. Of the things that had to be bought, Auntie had more, but of the things that were grown, we had plenty. We shared stuff back and forth. If your neighbor happens to be less fortunate than you are, give to them and don't give expecting anything back. God, in His infinite wisdom and infinite grace, will make sure that you get back everything that you are due. Auntie didn't give the cup of sugar because she was expecting Daddy to buy her a sack, but nevertheless, when Daddy returned the sugar, he didn't just return her a cup. He brought her an entire sack of sugar!

We don't have to be intimidated or timid about people being around us who need something from us. It's actually a privilege to be able to give. Auntie had to have something in order for her to give something to us. Would you rather be the person asking or the person who is giving? I'll take giving any day of the week. When God knows that if you have it, you will release it to whoever needs it, then He will let you have it.

So many days I come into the sanctuary, and people will put money in my hands, and nine times out of ten when people put money in my hands, it's because God has already shown me that I need to give somebody something, and so he provides it through one of the saints because He knows I'll pass it on. Hallelujah! Praise God! It just blesses others to see how God made a provision for them in a way that they knew only God could have done. We should be really rejoicing when people need something from us. It's a time to rejoice. Can you get excited when people need something and you are in a place to provide? Do you see it differently now? Can't you just see how blessed you are? No matter what you are lacking, can't you see how blessed you are if you're in a position to give to someone else? First of all, if your neighbor is your enemy, they are your provision. And secondly, if your neighbor is less fortunate than you are, you are to give to them.

Make Provision for Neighbors Who Are Wounded

And finally, let's look at Luke 10. This is a familiar passage of Scripture, the story of the Good

A Word on Love

Samaritan. What better story to relate to us how we should treat our neighbors:

And, behold, a certain lawyer stood up, and tempted him, saying, Master, what shall I do to inherit eternal life? He said unto him, What is written in the law? how readest thou? And he answering said, Thou shalt love the Lord thy God with all thy heart, and with all thy soul, and with all thy strength, and with all thy mind; and thy neighbour as thyself. And he said unto him, Thou hast answered right: this do, and thou shalt live. But he, willing to justify himself, said unto Jesus, And who is my neighbour? And Jesus answering said, A certain man went down from Jerusalem to Jericho, and fell among thieves, which stripped him of his raiment, and wounded him, and departed, leaving him half dead. And by chance there came down a certain priest that way: and when he saw him, he passed by on the other side. And likewise a Levite, when he was at the place, came and looked on him, and passed by on the other side. But a certain Samaritan, as he journeyed, came where he was: and when he saw him, he had compassion on him, And went to him, and bound up his wounds, pouring in oil and wine, and set him on his own beast, and brought him to an inn, and took care of him. And on the morrow when he departed, he took out two pence, and gave them to the host, and said unto him, Take care of him; and whatsoever thou spendest more, when I come again, I will repay thee. Which now of these three, thinkest thou, was neighbour unto him that fell among the thieves? And he said, He that shewed mercy on him. Then said Jesus unto him, Go, and do thou likewise. Now it came to pass, as they went, that he entered into a certain village: and a certain woman named Martha received him into her house. And she had a sister called Mary, which also sat at Jesus' feet, and heard his word. (Luke 10:25-39)

This wounded person is a passer-by. These passers-by don't live in the neighborhood. They're not people that we deal with every day. In fact, we may never see them again. It's easy to ignore a person that you don't even know and to choose not to get involved with. You can just tip your head just right so that it appears as if you don't see them. But God shows us here that this Samaritan made a conscious decision to get involved in this man's life. He didn't just get involved, either; he ended up procuring provisions for him. Now, your enemy will make provisions for you, and then you'll give to that person who really is in need; but this person is not only in need, they are down and out. This man was completely helpless and hopeless. He was left by the wayside to die. If you encounter someone like this, you should make a commitment to help this individual. Not only did the Samaritan *give* something to him, but he also *made provision* for his housing and he *made provision* for him to get to the location where he would receive care.

Once on a visit to the emergency room to help someone I know, I observed a young lady who was in excruciating pain. She was in so much in pain that she was agonizing and screaming in the middle of the waiting room and holding her stomach. I wasn't sure what was happening, but it was as if my body just left my seat, and before I knew it, I just got up to meet her. I said, *"Give me everything you have in your hand and come sit down,"* and I started asking her questions because I didn't know whether she was expecting, miscarrying, or what was going on. All I could tell was that she was in serious pain. My first question was, *"Are you pregnant? No? Okay, so you're not miscarrying..."* Then I just started asking some other questions, and she gave me some insight as to what was going on, but the reality of it was, there were a lot of sick people in that waiting room, but God said, *"Touch this one,"* so I just went to do that and in the process ended up having to go to the help counter and try to expedite her medical services.

The lady at the counter was so precious. She actually helped me! She knew that I didn't come there with the woman because she saw me when I came in with my acquaintances, but she said, "*Let me check...*" She checked the computer and said there was one room, but it was the room for the friend I had come in to see. I said, "*Well, she's obviously sick,*" so they gave her my friend's room and started to take care of her. I could have done nothing, but I was just too thankful to have the opportunity to make a provision. My friend was okay with allowing the woman in severe pain to receive services first. How many times are we in those environments like hospital waiting rooms and places where people are obviously in misery and pain, and all it takes is for us to just touch them?

After they brought her out for her next phase of treatment, she was feeling better! I said, "*To God be the glory!*" She didn't hear me pray, but of course, I did. I put my hands on her and I prayed for her even though I didn't know what she believed. I just needed her to be open to receive what God needed her to receive. When you do what you need to do with people who God puts in your hands to help, God gets all the glory. He gets all the praise and gets all the victory. I didn't give her my business card, and she doesn't know where to find me, because it wasn't about that. It was just about meeting the needs of one person that was in pain, doing for her what I would like somebody to do for me if I were in the same situation.

A Word on Love

Loving our neighbors is not complicated! If we just put ourselves in that person's place, we can make a sound decision. If you're sitting in agony, just the fact that someone comforts you can make the difference. At the time when I met this young lady, she was alone and needed some support. We see people every day and we know that they're walking alone. There may be crowds around them, but you can see in their spirit that they are alone and in need of a friendly, loving touch from you. They need a touch from God through your hands, and I'm here to say that your God will give you everything you need to meet that person's needs. The Good Samaritan said in verse 35, *"take care of him; and whatsoever thou spendest more, when I come again, I will repay thee."* He was in it for the long haul, not trying to get out of anything. How many of us would be willing to fork over our debit card and say, *"Whatever he needs, just put it on my account?"* Can you imagine what would happen if you did that? I've done it before, and I can tell you that you will see blessings and miracles galore!

When things are going haywire, God sustains us! If you offer an open purse to the needy, God will present an open purse to you, and you will see miracles happen in your own lives! Why? This is because you are loving your neighbors the way you should. Know that God will lead and direct you in the way you should go concerning meeting the needs of others.

Love is not a feeling. It is not a personality trait. It is not just a part of your character. It is willingly being led by the Spirit of God to do something that He wants you to do according to His Word. You must love God first and foremost. You must love yourself in a healthy way and you must love your neighbors.

A word on love? Love God with all that is within you and you will have the capacity to love according to His Word!

◆

A Word on Love

About the Author

Bishop Ruth W. Smith serves as Senior Pastor of Light of the World Christian Tabernacle International in Stockbridge, Georgia. She received her Masters Degree in Biblical Counseling in 2007 and her Doctorate of Ministry in 2008 from Biblical Life College and Seminary in Marshfield, Missouri. She has five children and ten grandchildren who fully support her ministry.

Bishop Ruth and her late husband, Archbishop Jimmie L. Smith, developed the Light of the World Interdenominational International Association, a non-profit Christian organization with a membership of over 200,000 in 13 different countries, and Bishop Ruth currently serves as Presiding Prelate.

Bishop Ruth is known throughout the world as a "Messenger with a Word in Season" and has become a world traveler sharing her gifts of administration, teaching and pastoring.

CONTACT INFORMATION

For appearances and upcoming event information, please contact Bishop Ruth Ministries:

5883 Highway 155 North, Stockbridge, GA 30281
678-565-7001 askrws@aol.com

◆

ORDER FORM

Return with your check or money order to
Excellent Way Enterprises, P. O. Box 421 Lithonia, GA 30058

Catalog Information

BRM001	A Word on Love	$14.95
CDD001	Sing with Me: Bible ABCs	$19.95
CDD002	Sing with Me: Bible 123s	$19.95

QTY	ORDER #	TITLE	UNIT PRICE	TOTAL PRICE

Ship. (Quant.) 1-5   6-10   11-15   16-29
Ship. Cost $5.00 $10.00 $12.00 $15.00

SUBTOTAL

Note: For orders of 30 or more, call EWE to speak to a
representative from the wholesale division.

SHIPPING

Name: _____

Address: _____

TOTAL DUE

City/State/Zip: _____

Date: _____ Phone: _____

Payment Information

Card Type: VISA MasterCard Discover

Card #: _____ Exp.: _____

Email: _____

To order additional copies:

- Mail order form to the address above along with check or money order
- Fax order form to 770-217-3135
- Call EWE at 770-899-2851 to provide order and payment details
- Visit www.excellentwayenterprises.com to order and pay online

Contact EWE at 770-899-2851 for additional book titles and upcoming releases.

THANK YOU FOR YOUR BUSINESS

LaVergne, TN USA
01 April 2010
177880LV00002B/1/P